OCTOBER'S CHILD

OCTOBER'S CHILD

Poems

DOT KILLIAN

FLOATING LEAF PRESS
CHARLOTTE, NORTH CAROLINA

Thanks to the editors/publishers of the following in which these writings first appeared:

"Two Old Women" was published in *Black Poetry of the '80s from the Deep South: Word Up*. (Beans & Brown Rice, Atlanta, GA)

"Homecoming" was published in *The Ivy Leaf*. (The magazine of Alpha Kappa Alpha Sorority, Inc.)

"Had We Known" was published in *A Living Culture in Durham*. (Carolina Wren Press, Durham, NC)

Front cover photograph and author photograph by Linda F. Kennedy

Library of Congress Control Number:2019914254
ISBN 978-1-950499-05-2

Published in the United States of America by
Floating Leaf Press
A division of
WordPlay
Maureen Ryan Griffin
6420 A-1 Rea Road, Suite 218
Charlotte, NC 28277

DEDICATION

for my mother
Hilda V. Killian (1921-1981)
who loved me and encouraged me to see beyond
the walls; whose love for words and knowledge
coupled with her love for people and laughter
and God inspired me to walk in her light.

and to
Beaunetta Brice Glenn (Net) (1917-2001)
who loved me with such amazing love and gave
me every ounce of her attention and her warm
hugs which shall forever remain in my heart.

and to
Linda F. Kennedy
whose love, encouragement and support through
all these years have given me the confidence
and the courage to do and to be the person that
God has called me to be.

and to
Adrian, Kevin, Shanita, and Mercedes,
my godchildren,
who taught me to love unselfishly and to listen
with my heart.

TABLE OF CONTENTS

THE HEART OF MY YOUTH   1
HOOP CHEESE AND COOKIES   2
TAKE SOMETHING WITH YOU   5
MESSAGE IN THE RAIN   7
WRITTEN IN TIMES OF   8
1983 OR 1893   9
nothingnothingnothingnothingnothing   10
APPOINTMENT AT 1:00 P.M.   12
AS WE WATCH   13
YOU LEFT   14
FOR LYDIA AND ELIZA
WHOM I NEVER MET   15
HAD WE KNOWN   17
WRITTEN IN THE A.M.   20
AFTER THE FUNERAL   22
UNTITLED   23
TRAPPED   24
FOR AN EX-BOSS   25
THE DREAM DISSOLVES   26
I WILL TELL MY GRANDCHILDREN   27
TWO CHILDREN PLAYING IN MUD   28
HOMECOMING   29
TWO OLD WOMEN   34
THE CLARINET LINE   35
I LOVE YOU   38
YES!   39
BEACH MEMORIES   40
LETTER TO A FRIEND   41

WINTER THOUGHTS   43

WE ARE BROKEN; YET, WE ARE WHOLE   44

ODE TO A DEAD BROTHER   46

MUSINGS   48

FOR LOU   49

FOR DAD   51

THE SHIP OF LIFE   53

THE BEACH IN OCTOBER   55

AS YOU JOURNEY HOME   57

A DREAM FULFILLED   59

GRATITUDE   62

THE HEART OF MY YOUTH

The heart of my youth grows with the sun,
becomes thrilled with the cry of a baby,
disillusioned with the promises of politicians.

Life empties itself onto the screened porch
never asking for direction or reason.
We are inundated with our own peculiarities
while we smother ourselves in our productivity.

The grass grows tall in the fields of our memory,
we forget names and smiles and dreams.
The heart of my youth grows with the sun,
Endlessly.

HOOP CHEESE AND COOKIES

I, or rather we, called him "Uncle." In fact, all the neighborhood children who came to our house called him "Uncle," just like they called his wife "Aunt Nannie," and her sister "Aunt Mamie."

Aunt Mamie was the only woman I have ever seen smoke a pipe, and she did it without any compromise to her femininity. Truth be told, she smoked it with great style.

Aunt Mamie was a thin dark-skinned woman who kept herself and everything around her super neat. She used to sweep our dirt yard and then rake it so the print of the rake would leave a pattern in the dirt.

She planted red and yellow and purple forget-me-nots in old car tires. She wore starched dresses and a starched apron with a pocket where she kept her money; she always had money. She read the newspaper from cover to cover and again. They say I take after Aunt Mamie.

Aunt Nannie was a light-skinned woman who had diabetes and ate nasty tasting bread and who drank Diet-Rite colas. Aunt Nannie liked to sit in the swing at the end of the porch, so that she could spit her snuff onto the ground.

Uncle, Aunt Nannie's husband, was a tall thin no-nonsense man who loved to sit on our front porch with his walking cane next to his chair. His real name was Thompson Glenn but we called him "Uncle."

The cane was used for walking, but it was sometimes used to grab wayward children who were cussing or fighting.

Uncle wore cotton trousers with snap-on suspenders and a leather belt. He smoked a cigar or a pipe with Prince Albert's tobacco. Although he wore his collar buttoned all the way to the neck, you could still see his long johns sticking out at the top. He wore long johns year 'round. His shoes were either black or brown lace ups and he loved to eat watermelon.

When the watermelon truck came, me and Uncle would walk out to the edge of the yard and Uncle would ask the man what he was asking for the watermelons. The man knew that Uncle would never pay the asking price. He would say, "3 for $5.00." Uncle would say, "I'll give you $4.00 for 4 watermelons."

The man would agree.

Uncle always got to get a half of the
watermelon. He didn't really eat it. He would
suck the juice out and spit the watermelon and
the seeds into a long black pan on his lap.

Uncle used to take me to Mr. Wheeler's store to
buy hoop cheese and cookies and Pepsi. You
could get 50 cookies for a quarter and a
quarter's worth of hoop cheese and two Pepsis
and still have change out of a dollar.

Me and Uncle would walk
back down the dusty street
to our house. Me,
a little nappy-haired girl
with a sweater on in July.
He, a tall thin man with
snap-on suspenders
and a leather belt.

We didn't say anything to
each other, but we knew
that once we hit that front
porch, we were going to
give that hoop cheese,
them two-for-a-penny
Jack's cookies,
and them Pepsis
 a run for their money.

TAKE SOMETHING WITH YOU

As you pass gracefully into womanhood
into a new and exciting awareness of
who you are and how you came to be that way,
take something with you.

As you grow from adolescence into adulthood
and as you begin to have some understanding of
the vastness of the world and the myriad
opportunities that await your generation,
take something with you.

As you follow your dreams to places
and possibilities which are still buried
in your imagination; as you fulfill the promises
and expectations of your kindred
and all who watched you grow,
take something with you.

As you become the leaders of a powerful
and diverse nation; as you seek to unravel
mysteries locked away for centuries
from your ancestors and mine,
take something with you.

Take LOVE, take HUMILITY, take DISCIPLINE,
take an undying thirst for KNOWLEDGE,
WISDOM, and UNDERSTANDING. Take HOPE,
take PRIDE in your HERITAGE,

take RESPECT for yourselves and for humankind and for the environment.

Take COMPASSION, take SINCERITY and HONESTY, take PERSERVERANCE, take FAITH, take TIME, take the LOVE OF GOD.
TAKE CHARGE!

MESSAGE IN THE RAIN

There is a message in the rain. Listen to it call
out to your soul.
It tells of days and years gone
and ones to come.
Listen, listen as the clear cool drops splash on
the newly waxed Chevy.
Raindrops, Raindance, find your corner and hear
the words and feelings of
the rain.

The wind blows the rain against my face. Fogged
glasses dim my view of the universe.
The message, though, is etched firmly
in my breast.
My feet dance at the feeling of the soggy earth
between my toes.

Rain brings a message to the earth. It cleanses
the fruit, the grasses, and the creatures
Who, like me, should listen.
There is a message in the rain. Listen to it call
out to your soul.

WRITTEN IN TIMES OF

Bullets!
Killing all the young men. Mothers left alone to
rear the young.
Daddies gone off to fight the white man's war.
Black folk being shot down by CON-SER-VA-TIVE
RE-PUB-LI-CAN PO-LICE-MEN who don't like
"niggers" anyway.
Men flyin' 'round the moon in rockets in our
nation of plenty.
PLENTY OF HATRED
PLENTY OF POVERTY
PLENTY OF RACISM
PLENTY OF HUNGER
PLENTY OF POLITICIANS
Who tell me they 'gon make everything alright.

1983 OR 1893

The eyes are unkind in a kind way, trying to
mask the bias that eats at the soul.

The forced smile pushes through the scowl which
was not supposed to be detected.

"Why I love coloreds. Theys as nice
as they can be."

The moment arrives when illusions must give
way to reality. The cries of forgiveness trail off,
never reaching the ears of a deaf black Jesus.

nothingnothingnothingnothingnothing

They are not all black men. Some are old men.
Some are young men, very young.
They all have the same despair.
Their eyes half-looking, half-seeing
to avoid the curious stares
of the noontime bureaucrats,
their eyes sharing
a common theme of hopelessness.

Their dirty ill-fitting clothes, their struggling gait
bind them together like
a revolutionary army going to fight a major war,

EXCEPT

Their government forgot to give them weapons
for war.
They have a common smell of urine and vomit
and sweat.
They beg for cigarettes, for change,
for attention.
I smile politely hoping not to appear
too unfriendly.

What separates me from them?
Nothingnothingnothingnothingnothing.

I sit and feel sorry for them after I treat myself
to a gourmet lunch at the Radisson.
I sit and write poetry about them with my
expensive pen and my legal pad,
Gloating at my sense of civic duty
and responsibility.

What separates me from them?
Nothingnothingnothingnothingnothing

Meanwhile the intellectual me reads the *Wall
Street Journal, Forbes,* and *Law Week* knowing
that my future is secure as I cash my paycheck
and plan outings to the beach with my children.

I pretend not to know, not to see, not to
understand the pain in the eyes of a man
who must hold his faded, tattered, oversized
jeans up with a rope because he has no belt.
That same man picks up a cigarette butt from
the sidewalk. He asks if I have a light.
I politely shake my head, "No."

APPOINTMENT AT 1:00 P.M.

We will be in touch with you as soon as we check
to see whether we have already met our quota
of coloreds and nigras and women
who have such impressive resumés and, my,
you do have a great deal of experience, but we
are looking for someone whose background
is closer
to the job description . . . you understand the
overrated supervisor who is afraid of challenge
and tries to hide his racism behind his pot belly
and green contact lens which blink impishly at
the mahogany desk of files and reasons why we
try to find qualified coloreds who understand the
system which belongs to them too because
we want to give them a chance to prove
themselves, but we are limited by funds and
rules and laws
that I am sure you read about in school when
you were studying to be a lawyer and learning
that there is not very much difference in
a 39-year-old black woman with a huge Afro
and who has a master's degree and a law degree
and one with a second grade education is really
the key to the future if you just believe that you
can change the mind and heart of the oppressor
you are really a fool who needs to learn the
other rules that are not printed in the book
review section of the *New York Times.*

AS I WATCH

Changing in the wake of turmoil can cause
undue stress on the mind which relentlessly
seems to border
on insanity.

Crisis seems to be the norm as we rush to meet
the deadline only to find that another looms
ahead.

Our dreams, once our friends, now become our
enemies as we watch cruel realties position
themselves at our doorstep.

As they carry the banners of pride and equality
and reach for magnificent tranquility, we watch
along the distant shores hoping for a tomorrow.

YOU LEFT

When you left me, you said it was because I
wore my hair too short, too nappy,
'cause I talked too loud, didn't pronounce my
ed's and my s's properly, and 'cause I
couldn't cook like yo' mama, and 'cause I didn't
appreciate your accomplishments.
Well, my hair has grown longer, and I have
invested in a most effective perm. I have
adjusted my tone of voice, and I have learned to
pronounce my ed's and my s's properly. I
learned to cook. I can't cook like yo' mama and I
do appreciate your accomplishments.
So, where are you?
Still hiding behind hair and voice and food and
language and your accomplishments and
yourself.
Come out from your misery. Give way to truth.
You left because you wanted to. I left because I
had to.

FOR LYDIA AND ELIZA WHOM I NEVER MET

Strong-willed
Song-filled
Hatred-killed

Women of my bones
Your ghosts and their sisters cry out at my
complacency, but I have not forgotten
the lashes. I, too, bear the scars of the
"institution." I feel the same scorn
beating down on
my head even as they smile politely. I still hear
your voices and I promise to heed them.
I will not become enchanted with illusions and
other falsities, for I know that your dreams must
be carried on my back to the next generation
and the next. Your prayers for freedom are yet
prayed by
me and all of us who love you.
You have given me the hope that was yours,
and I have fed from the breast of your children.
I have received the love and the strength
that you gave to me through them.

HAD WE KNOWN

I sat in the cool quiet room drinking *Coca-Cola*
watching the magnificent games. I thought of
the days when I was an Olympian . . . kinda.

We used to run and jump and play without
fanfare or Adidas running gear. We yelled
and screamed and cheered when somebody hit
a homerun defined by imaginary boundaries.

I saw the beauty of Los Angeles, the city of
angels, the coliseum, the arena, the crowd.

I thought of our "venue," as the announcer
called it:
Mud-puddled yards, dirt streets, grassy vacant
fields. Our equipment, most original. Balls
fashioned from a white baby doll's head. Our
bat, a 2x4, quite possibly from somebody's
house or outhouse.

I watched the splendor of the gold being
presented to the victors. My mind reeled
backwards to the prizes of our games. If you
could shoot marbles better 'n anybody else,
you could win a big round heavy marble called
a "steel, or a big red and green and purple one
called "a aggie." Or if you was 'round my mama,
"an aggie." I owned neither.

We never knew that people actually won gold
and silver for playing, 'cause the only silver
we knew was the Lone Ranger's horse.

I smiled to myself as I watched the lithesome
gymnasts as they turned and hooked their
youthful bodies.

I thought about my painful and short-lived
attempts at ballet and tap. Somehow soft-toed
pink shoes aren't much fun to shoot marbles in.

I felt the blows thrown by the mighty and
powerful boxers. I thought about the blows
I had thrown and received.

One time I took a bat to the head of a classmate
during a softball game. Another time, a girl who
is now dead and who was bigger than me
knocked me down in red mud 'cause I wouldn't
let her use my souvenir pencil me and my mama
bought at the Elks parade in Washington, D.C.

In another battle (same venue) I hit a girl
with a bag of jaw breakers and got pinched
by the teacher who used her fingernails
as weapons.

I watched the beautiful colors of the flags,
the costumes, the faces. I went back to the
colors and faces and realities of my youth.

What if we had known about gymnastics then?
What if we had known about swimming
at the YMCA?
What if we had known that running
was actually a sport, and you didn't have to be
running from something or somebody?

I think perhaps the beauty of the games
is too much for me.
Somehow, I know that even as I cheer
the accomplishments of the Olympians
in every category, as I sing the National Anthem
with tears streaming down my face, I know
there is much more to it. Much, much more.

WRITTEN IN THE A.M.

The morning is for lovers who oft retire
themselves into shiftless oblivion,
falling prey to jubilance and feting, seeking
existence not to be recognized by humanity.
The morning gives essence, totality to the
scheme of things. Each minute measuring years
of incomparable fortitude.
The morning is for lovers. Serene, silent,
sensual. Nature's way of revealing herself. God's
way of unveiling the magnanimity of God's
divine power.

AFTER THE FUNERAL

It was not what you said or didn't say. It was not
what you did or didn't do.

Although I was excited about your decision to
attend the reading without prior notice, it was
not what you wore or didn't wear. The navy suit
did speak volumes about your style.

It was a sad time, yet some happiness grew out
of it. Old friendships were rekindled; new
friendships were born. We are to rejoice at
death, they say, and before the evening ended,
I did rejoice. You said that was the best time
that you'd had in a very long time.

Your temperament impressed me.
Your demeanor was alluring. The gray
in your hair . . . oh never mind.

I must remember that these are all false signs.
Middle age and loneliness and vulnerability and
grief, together with rain and poetry and shrimp
and expensive cologne and imported wine can
make for a rather complicated chain of events.

UNTITLED

Reaching out to touch you as though you were
there,
Reaching out to love you as though you were
there. Reaching out to hold you as though you
were there. Reaching out to warm you as though
you were there.
Instead of you, I found
An untouchable
Unlovable
Unholdable
Unwarmable
Body
Pretending to be real.

TRAPPED

Comfortable
Yet
Cold
Yet
Hot
Cool Cool
Cool as can be
giving the appearance of
HAR-MO-NY and fun.
Feeling cheated, unanswered, un-understood.
Never being able to intellectualize. Just jive,
Trapped.

FOR AN EX-BOSS

There are dreams that die fast and then there
are those dreams that attach themselves
to your marrow and cling to you like a crab
clinging to the side of a pot of scalding water.

I cannot allow you to destroy my dreams,
for if I give you that power, you will conquer
my soul and my hope.

Your wisdom is tainted with foolish folly, but
your gamesmanship is superb.

The other players spotted you three paces
and left you alone to cross the finish line.
I came thinking victory, believing that together
we could crack the pot of gold.

My illusions have been shocked by a bald and
bare reality; your conscience has no boundaries.
Your arrogance has no limitations.

I will leave before you destroy
what I cherish most.
I will leave with my dreams intact.
I will leave with my soul pure and free.

THE DREAM DISSOLVES

The dream dissolves painlessly, gradually, as we
try and pretend it never was.

The mind remains the most formidable obstacle
encountered by emotion. No compromise
approaches the solution, least none has
surfaced.

There will be other times when these cares seem
idle and juvenile; yet, for now, we must strive
for resolve as we quietly die.

I WILL TELL MY GRANDCHILDREN

That I went to college and got my degree
and my master's degree and my law degree,
and I worked
hard and went to Sunday School
and went to the Olympics and sang
the National Anthem and served as a city judge
and planted flowers in my yard and visited
hospitals and funeral homes and then . . .

I went to the interview dressed in my good suit
and my good shoes and my good blouse
and having done all you're told to do, knowing
about the job and the employer and conversing
intelligently with the interviewer and then . . .

Finding out that Fredrick and Martin and Medgar
and Emmett Till and Harriet Tubman and Fannie
Lou Hamer and Malcolm and all the people who
died for freedom have been cheated and . . .

I came back to my house and prayed that I
would be able to tell my grandchildren about
love and hard work and hope and opportunity
and maybe this time it would be the truth.

TWO CHILDREN PLAYING IN MUD

I passed two children the other day. Rain was pouring down and the children ran from behind a dilapidated house and began to run through the rain with reckless abandonment as only children can.

Oh, to be able to play in mud again; to walk barefoot and let the mud squish up between your toes . . .

There is much joy and laughter as the two children play in the mud without care or purpose.

I watched the children playing and then the light was green, and my world of fantasy was abruptly shattered. I drove away in awe and with a huge smile.

Two children playing in mud. Some things never change. Some things should never change.

HOMECOMING

The country brings back memories of childhood,
of sweet flower buds, of bumblebee stings,
of blackberries.
I can see the old country church, rocking to
the rhythms of a hundred voices present
and a thousand souls past.
Fat ladies in wide-brimmed hats with feathers
and bananas on the top.
Sweat pouring down their necks, singing
the praises, though never understanding
the husband who drank too much and worked
too little.
Ushers dressed in starched white uniforms, ruby
red lipstick, hair straightened with *Royal Crown
Pressing Oil*, black patent leather pumps with red
fox stockings, passing out fans with pictures of
Jesus and Martin Luther King on the back.
Passing out smelling salts to those overcome by
the heat or by the Holy Ghost or both.

My grandfather is there . . . tall, stately,
gold watch chain, vested suit, trousers creased
sharp enough to cut a slab of bacon. He,
authoritatively, directs the cars into
the tiny dirt-filled parking lot.
Big Meeting Sunday. Cousins and aunts and
uncles known and unknown fill
the tiny wooden pews.

A baby screams; an usher rushes him outside
to less frantic surroundings.
Outside the church, women and children are
working feverishly over a long wooden table
filled with Ms. Minnie Simpson's egg custard,
country ham, potato salad, green beans, and
pound cake sent by Sister Jessie Mae
Cunningham who don't get 'round much since
her cataract operation.

There seems to be a quiet peace around the
table despite the sounds coming from inside.
The country brings back memories of a life gone
by; of a people whose love keeps us constant
amidst the turmoil of modernity.

KILLIAN FAMILY REUNION 2002

REMEMBERING OUR HERITAGE

AUGUST 30-SEPT 1 2002
CHESTER, SOUTH CAROLINA

MEMORIAL BANQUET
SEPTEMBER 1, 2002 3:00 P.M.
CHURCH OF GOD OF PROPHECY
FAMILY LIFE CENTER
CHESTER, SOUTH CAROLINA

PROGRAMME

GREETINGS/WELCOME	ODESSA MOORE MARSHALL
SCRIPTURE	ROBERT EARL KILLIAN
PRAYER	GEORGE J. KILLIAN
SELECTION	THE FAMILY
FAMILY INTRODUCTIONS	PATRICIA MOORE
CANDLE LIGHTING CEREMONY	DOROTHY JEAN KILLIAN
	GEORGE W. KILLIAN, JR.
	DENZELL MARSHALL
FAMILY HISTORY	JOE ARTHUR KILLIAN
SELECTION	THE FAMILY
SPECIAL TRIBUTE	GREGORY KILLIAN
REMARKS	GEORGE W. KILLIAN, JR.

-----DINNER-----

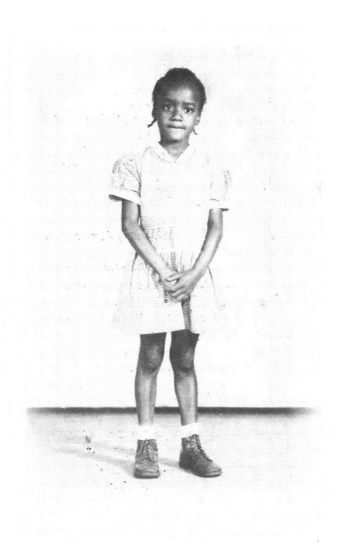

TWO OLD WOMEN

Two old women sat on the shore of a huge lake,
one on a folding chair,
the other on a black lard bucket.
They sat patiently making small talk
about the weather and the swiftness
of the water.

"B'lieve I got a bite." The fatter of the two
women flipped her pole out of the water.
Something had taken her bait and left a string of
a worm on the hook.
"I'll get that rascal," she mumbled to herself and
to her fishing partner.

Hours passed. The sun made its way to
its bedroom on the western shore.
Crickets began their mindless chirping
as the water receded and evening
peeped out from between the tall trees.

The two old women as though synchronized
got up from their respective perches, gathered
their belongings and headed for home.

"Where we gon' fish tomorrow?"
"Don't know yet, but we gon' fish somewhere."

THE CLARINET LINE

(in memory of Wilma)

We were in the fifth grade at West End School
and all we cared about were lunch and boys.
You could get any boy to buy your lunch, but
you liked Hook Poag 'cause he always had
money to buy lunch.

We had begged our parents for clarinets
and, finally, we got them. Bright, shiny sleek
black and silver clarinets. Now we could be
in the District Three Elementary Band.
White pants, white shirts, white shoes, blue
corduroy capes, red on the reverse side. Bessie,
Mary, Dot & Wilma, Boyd Hill's finest. We formed
the clarinet line.

We used to walk to band practice at
Emmett Scott during the summer. You were
the tallest and the prettiest, so we would let you
walk out front ahead of us and get a ride
from some unsuspecting guy who thought
he was picking up a mature lady.
As soon as he pulled over, you would yell,
"Come on, y'all," and me and Mary and Bessie
would run and hop in the car
much to the man's disappointment.

We were inseparable. We played the clarinet. We
sang in the eighth-grade talent show, and then
we took our show on the road to Friendship
College. We were Diana Ross and the Supremes.

And then the magic began. 1962. Emmett Scott
High School Marching Band. We wore our blue
and gold uniforms with tremendous pride.
You were the only one who cared about your
lipstick and your hair while we were marching.
The clarinet line. Now there were six of us. Mary,
Bessie, Willie Ruth, Wilma Dot, Patricia. We were
the last line in the band. The grand finale!

And then you were Miss Homecoming and then
we graduated, and you were injured.
Then you could no longer walk or march
in the clarinet line.

And then you survived with the same love of life
and the same concern for your Mama and Daddy
and your grandmama and Snow and William
and Fannie and Donna and Dwight
and Everett . . . and especially Fernando.
Oh, how you loved Fernando!

And then we lost you, but not before you were
crowned Miss Wheelchair South Carolina, and
not before you competed in the Miss Wheelchair
USA pageant, and not before you were featured
in the Herald, and not before you graduated

from Winthrop University with both graduate
and undergraduate degrees, and not before you
developed a strong and abiding faith in God
and a personal relationship with Jesus Christ.

That is why we are able to celebrate your life,
your love, your spirit.

We send you home now, so that you can have
more time to see that your hair is in place,
and your lipstick and your shoes match
your dress, so that you can get ready to march
in the new clarinet line in glory.

I LOVE YOU

I love you, but we've tried love. Love was not
enough. Still, I love you. All of me loves you.
I need to see your face and bury my tears in
your eyes and make peace with you and us.
I need to love you again and try and understand
your fear and your tears.

But you are not mine. Never shall be again, and
as much as I love you, I surrender you, us, all,
for your peace and contentment,

Many, many years will pass and my love for you
will remain, but our lives will go on and our
paths will never cross again. You asked, and I
promised to forget.

The days ahead. What holds for us? Who knows?
Who cares? Who is? Who was?
Keep all you need and destroy the rest.
May the angels encircle you forever.

YES!

Somewhere along the tumultuous path of love
and loss and pain and depression, I knew
that I wanted to have you again.
This time it had nothing to do with possession
or obsession.
It had to do with you and me, two human beings
in love.

I called your sister and told her
that I wanted to try again.
She listened patiently and offered
her suggestions for consummating the plan.
"Wait," she said. "Wait. Then, pick up the
telephone and say where you are and wait.
Then you'll know from there."

I waited. 30 days, 60 days, 90 days, and on
the 100th day, I sent 43 red roses, 42 for
each year of your life and one for our singular
life together as one couple, one agenda,
one home, one love, one family.

You came crying and laughing at once. We held
each other and without any words, we knew
then as we know now that the answer had been
decided long before this teary evening.
Yes!

BEACH MEMORIES

Through the years they made their annual
pilgrimage to the seashore
From far, from near they came sharing food
and wine and laughter and tears.
Each brought stories of lost love and found love,
of childhood fears and grown-up frustrations.
Each felt a lifetime of pain and anguish
at the water's edge.

At first there was much merrymaking,
games and dancing and vodka tonics.
Later the mood grew somber, almost
melancholy.
The passing of years tempered the laughter.
The passing of loved ones touched each soul.

Every year the journey became more arduous.
Names changed, partners changed, people
moved further away, until it was finally no more.
There were no good-byes, many regrets, many
joys, many tears.

But even yet, the sea awaits their return
in October.
Perhaps someday they will return with
their grandchildren and their games and their
laughter.

LETTER TO A FRIEND

I feel so helpless, so singly incapable of rescuing
you from this terrible demon that has invaded
your body.

I ached when I received the awful news on my
birthday, that eight days before, the angel of
death had posted himself at your bedside.
I cried so hard, wondering why, wondering
when, wondering how this manifestation of evil
would leave the earth.

I did not know that you were ill. I did not know
that you were dying. I did not know that you
were penniless. I did not know that you were
homeless or family-less until . . .

A friend called to wish me a Happy Birthday.
During the conversation, she said, "I guess
you heard about Phillip."
Had I known, I asked myself, what would I
have done? Now that I know, what will I do?

Will I try and find your chilly corpse and return it
to the soil of your boyhood? Will I erect a living
memorial for you in my law office? Will I visit
your unmarked grave and weep as I drop pink
rose petals on your head?

Will I read a poem in your memory at our next
class reunion as I have done for classmates who
died before, or . . .?

Will I forget your anguish? Dismiss your smile
with the gleaming gold crown? Deny our
weekend trips to Atlanta with $15.00
and a Citgo gas card? Escape the questions
of uncaring and unsympathetic classmates?

I miss the expectancy of seeing you even though
we hadn't seen each other in years.
Despite my pain, I know that you are free.
I know that whatever good there is in death,
you will wring every single ounce of it until death
screams and pleads with you, "Let me go!"

WINTER THOUGHTS

Spinning
     the words and watching them unread on
the tables of the mind

Watching
     the glow flicker like a wet match in the
breath of the wind

Feeling
     the spirit wander into realms of
nothingness

Knowing
     that life and love are essentially the
same though they
     often pretend that they have never met.

WE ARE BROKEN; YET, WE ARE WHOLE

(in loving memory of Aunt Mag)

Our hearts are broken, our tears flow like rivers
through years of love and joy and laughter.
Our grief covers our smiles and our fears.
Our dreams are broken, shattered like crystal
thrown against concrete walls, pieces
tossed about onto seas of loneliness.

Our homes are broken. The void can never
be filled. We struggle for composure looking
to heaven for answers.
Finding strength in God's promise
and in each other.

Our hears are broken; our dreams are broken;
our homes are broken; yet, we are whole.

We are whole because of who she was
and what she gave to us. We are whole because
of her courage and her strength.
We are whole because of her selfless devotion
to our family.
We are whole because she is now secure
and at peace.

We are broken; yet, we are whole.

CHESTER
MAY 10
1943
S.C.

THIS SIDE OF CARD IS FOR ADDRESS

Miss Hilda V. Killian
Friendship College
Rock Hill
South Carolina

all the family er
OK Love J
Finley H. School
Chester S.C.
May 10, 1943

Dear Hilda,
I wrote you a letter
this morning I guess
you have received it
by now. I am in the
P.O. Writing this card
it is raining very hard
I want you to let me use
your pink evening dress
please. We will need them
the 19th of May I would
like to have it as quick
as you can bring it.
ans. soon
your sister
Magdalene

ODE TO A DEAD BROTHER

I cannot weep for your funeral cortege, for it will
pass through streets unknown,
Just as we passed through moons and stars
of mystery.
You were a victim of your soul's search for
happiness made
unattainable by the expectations
of your kindred.
We knew that what our father did to our mothers
was unjustifiable,
but we loved him still.

Your children will never know you as I knew you.
Their measurements were tainted with false
and foolish comparisons.
I watch them and wish that they could somehow
understand who you really were.

You were who you wanted to be; yet, you longed
to be someone else.

The last time I saw you rings clear in my mind.
I bought a bottle of
bourbon for you knowing
that its contents were compounding
your misery.

But your eyes and your non-smile told me that
you had given up on this world, and
that you were ready to seek a new world.

I cannot sit in the solemn pews as they eulogize
your remains,
for they will not speak truth but will utter sweet
fabrications.
The father of our youth awaits you. Spend time
with him and perhaps
he can tell you why he left so many
of our questions unanswered.

MUSINGS

We live our lives like rose petals dropping
to the floor of the moist rusted basement,
Looking to see if purple moonglows caught
a glimpse of our fading shadows.
Days are spent pondering loss . . . lost people,
lost trust, lost hope.
We see winged birds on the roof tops of ample
houses; yet we doubt that
Birds can really fly without some divine
intervention.

Children's laughter annoys rather than delights
us. We push the labels backward and
claim anonymity and celebrity at once,
as though they are the same.
We stir in the pot of avoidance until we are set
face to face with our fears.

Where are the days of church bells ringing
on Sunday mornings and puppies running
out to meet the school bus?
Where are the mommies who brought home
Tootsie Roll Pops to soothe a runny nose?

FOR LOU

(Mary Louise Barnette was born
on March 14, 1948,
in Rock Hill, South Carolina.
Lou died on December 13, 2003,
in Atlanta, Georgia, of cancer.)

I think I knew, we both knew
That the prayer we prayed together
on October 22 would be our last.
We knew that God's plan for your life had been
revealed, painful, yet clear.
You asked me to read the long and ominous
report about the clinical trial.
Nothing in it gave us hope.
I cried as I drove away from your house. I knew
that I would never see you alive again.

Through the tears, I remembered your head,
bald, scalp smooth without a blemish.
I read scripture to you that morning
seeking to comfort you and me in that moment
of uncertainty.
We had put you in the bathtub the night before,
but nothing stopped the pain.

You never complained about the pain that
wracked your body without pause.

You sounded cheery over the phone
for the benefit of the caller. Some people never
knew that you were dying because you didn't
want them to worry.

You told me that you wanted
to come home for Christmas.
You did.
We returned your body as you requested
to the dirt and grass of your youth,
Mt. Hebron Baptist Church.

We said farewell quietly at the graveside without
fanfare as you told us to.
Adrian and Chase and Charlie sat on the front
row side by side. You would have been
 proud of them.

We were all there. Dad stayed in the funeral car.
We all closed our eyes and you were gone.
Then the preacher said, "Amen."

FOR DAD

Through the years your laughter rang out
in the house and in our hearts. Your love for
Mom and Cecil, Frankie, Calvin and Louise
was immeasurable.

And then there was Adrian who stole your heart,
and who was the joy of your life.
You gave Adrian all the love you had
and then some. You taught him courage
and hard work and faith and responsibility.

You taught me and Calvin and Louise and
Frankie how to enjoy cabbage and pig feet
on rainy Saturday afternoons.
We pretended to be watching Wide World
of Wrestling with you, but we would always
convince Mom to let us go back into the kitchen
to get more cabbage.

You taught us to endure loss and heartbreak,
pain and loneliness. We watched your smile
and your laughter slowly disappear as we said
good-bye to Mom, and Calvin, and Louise
and then to Frankie. Even as we watched you
tend your plant and eat KFC and chocolate candy
and drink Pepsi, Adrian and I sensed
that you had made plans to meet Mom
at the river's edge.

No long good-byes. No sorrowful sighs. You went
peacefully and quietly to be with the God
of your salvation.

We will remember the laughter that rang out
in the house and in our hearts. We will cherish
our time together, forever.

THE SHIP OF LIFE

(written in memory of Frankie Barnette)

The ship sets sail amidst seas of uncertainty
and gusts of expectation
winding through waves of doubt and despair.

A bird whispers to the captain that there are
smooth waters southward and the ship
navigates through warm breezes and exotic
rainforests.

The ship winds its way through rivers of promise
and hope and affirmation.

Sometimes it encounters dark and lonely
passageways littered with tears
and long good-byes.

Oftentimes, hard cold rains batter the ship
on every side.

The sails blow furiously as the captain struggles
to keep the vessel upright.

The night is bitter and raw, and the darkness
seems to extend beyond the earth and sky.

There in the distance, a small but radiant light appears. The ship turns and sails toward the light, passing through magnificently calm and pristine waters.

Finally, the ship drops anchor. The journey is over. Welcome home, my brother. Welcome home.

THE BEACH IN OCTOBER

There was a time when the beach in October
was secluded. Parents and screaming
two-year-olds and irritable teenagers having
departed for more structured living.

After they left, we found out what fun it was
to sit at the ocean's door and peek out
at the sunrise and feel the chilly breeze blow
against our windbreakers.

We always knew that there was something
different about the laughter and the fellowship.

We didn't know why but we gave credit to fresh
seafood and homemade biscuits.

So many memories both good and bad.
None so great as the first time; none so painful
as the last.

We knew that ours was fading,
and the beach in October would soon be like
tulips and gardenias in winter.

I went back to the beach today. I saw cool,
windy water and inviting sand.
I saw old friends and met new friends.
I ate fresh seafood and homemade biscuits.

I sat at the ocean's edge with the chilly breeze blowing against my face.

I returned home with fond memories and a heart filled with immeasurable pain.

AS YOU JOURNEY HOME

(for Stanley)

Through the years, we've traveled
many roads together,
To basketball games, to football games,
to fish at Santee,
To buy you a shorts set for your birthday,
to eat shrimp and ribs, to bid
loved ones farewell.
We shared great fun and laughter then, believing
that there would always be
time for another trip.

Yesterday, you left without us.
Although we were there trying desperately
to keep you here with us,
you whispered through the voice of angels
that this was a journey
that you had to take without us.

Even as the heavenly chariot came to carry
your smiling spirit
from its mortal body, we watched in anguish
and joy knowing that
our journeys together were over, but that your
pain and suffering were
nearing an end.

As we watched you breathe your last breath,
we knew that at the same time you were
breathing your first breath
in the great bedroom in
the sky.

As you journey home, go sweetly.
You won't have to stop and ask for directions
(not that you would anyway)
The way has already been prepared for you
thousands of journeys ago.

As you journey home, go peacefully.
As you journey home, go gently,
As you journey home, go with the assurance
that all of our journeys
together will never be quite as glorious as your
journey now.
As you journey home, go with our love.

A DREAM FULFILLED

(written to commemorate the 25th anniversary
of the Scott-ites)

We came from places of love, places of hope,
places of despair, places of joy,
places of expectation.
We came as fretful, whiny, self-conscious
adolescents, joined together in a flurry of
football games, basketball games, High School
Chorus, French Club, Typing, Baseball, Home
Economics, Glee Club, Marching Band,
Homecoming Queens, and Future Farmers
of America.

We came from Mt. Zion, New Zion, and Blue
Buckle. We came from Freidheim Road, Crawford
Road and Ogden Road. We came from Carolina
Avenue, Berry Street, Bynum Avenue,
Washington Court and Main Street. We came
from the Mill Hill, Flint Hill, and Boyd Hill. We
came from Sunset Park, and Cedar Oak Park,
and Twitty Court, Whit-Green, and Stroupe
Street, and Black Street and Porter Road and
places where there were no streets or roads.

We came from everywhere, searching to find
something greater than ourselves.

We came searching for answers. We came
looking for purpose and meaning in our lives.
We came hoping to find our own voices, our own
dreams, our own souls, our own way.

We came with excitement and enthusiasm even
in the midst of the jangling chords of oppression
and discrimination and segregation and lynching
and Jim Crow that shaped our world.

We came seeking new possibilities that our
mothers and fathers and our grandparents never
knew. We came seeking new truths for ourselves
and for our children and their children.

Our search led us through endless waves of
encouragement and support from our teachers.
We were respected; we were disciplined; we
were told that there were no limitations, and
that our wildest imaginations could become our
realities. We believed every word!

And here we are. Look at us! Beautiful,
intelligent, blessed people. We have searched
and we have found that all we need is within us.
We have searched and we have found that all we
have is a gift from Almighty God.

We are thankful to God for our searching. We
are thankful to God for our journey, a journey

that took us through the halls of our Alma Mater,
Emmett Scott High School.
We are assured that as long as we live,
Emmett Scott High School lives!

GRATITUDE

We can never know where roads will lead.
Sometimes we learn too late that the curve
in the road which seemed manageable was
actually a cliff.

So, we move along, hoping, wishing that
the pain will melt away and that we will become
like winged birds and fly over all the destruction
and breathe again.

There are always warning signs before danger
strikes; yet, we close our eyes and our minds
and allow our hearts to lead the way. Then we
come face to face with the danger announced by
the signs and we pretend not to notice.

My life has been forever changed. I have sat
at the entrance of death. It had to be God who
snatched me back so that I could live to write
this note of thanks.

Your love has made all the difference between
despair and delight.

Words fall short, but I want you to know
that I am eternally grateful for your love,
for your kindness, for your patience, for your
compassion, for your spirit, for you.

Thank you.

Made in the
USA
Lexington, KY